WHAT HAPPEI

1940

This journal is part of a series of "What Happened During The Year Of Your Birth" books available at
www.brightandbold.com

The information provided in this book was accurate as of the writing, however we take no responsibility for errors or omissions. It is provided for historical & entertainment purposes only.

BORN IN 1940?

Take a few moments to remember the year you were born and the sports teams, music, art, toys, movies & pop culture that made it a special year.

COST OF LIVING

Inflation Rate: 1.4%

Avg New Home: $3,920

Avg Annual Income: $1,725

Avg New Car: $850

Gas (per gallon): 11 cents

Loaf of bread: 10 cents

Gallon of milk: 34 cents

Dozen eggs: 34 cents

Postage stamp: 3 cents

Dow Jones Avg (Dec 31): 131

Minimum Wage (per hr): $ .30

Population of the USA: 132,120,000

POPULAR MOVIES

His Girl Friday, The Grapes Of Wrath, The Shop Around The Corner, Fantasia, The Letter, The Philadelphia Story, My Foreign Wife, The Seahawk

POPULAR MUSIC

Cliff Edwards, The Andrews Sisters, Buddy Clark, Frank Sinatra, Harvey Chermak, Bando Da Lua, The Ink Spots

POPULAR TV SHOWS

The Milton Berle Show, Kraft Television Theatre, The Lone Ranger, Arthur Godfrey's Talent Scouts, Martin Kane Private Eye

POPULAR TOYS

Erector sets, steel cars and trucks, doctor/nurse kits, military model plane kits, steel Radio Flyer wagons, tiddledywinks, kewpie dolls, phonographs

MAJOR EVENTS

Rearming of U.S. forces helps Great Depression impact to ease in U.S.

Nylon stockings invented in 1939 were all the rage with women

FDR was elected for a third term as President of the United States

Benjamin O. Davis, Sr becomes the first African-American General in U.S.

First peacetime military draft in U.S. history signed into law

Hattie McDaniel first African-American actor to win Academy Award

40 hour work week goes into effect

Walt Disney's animated film Pinocchio is released, along with Fantasia

The Narrows Suspension Bridge collapses in Tacoma, Washington

The Queen Mary, Mauritania & Queen Elizabeth Ocean Liners carry troops

SPORTING EVENTS

2nd NFL All Star Game, Green Bay Packers win

Joe Louis beats Arturo Godoy in 15 for heavyweight boxing title

First televised basketball game (U of Pittsburgh beats Fordham U)

NFL cuts clipping penalty from 25 yards to 15 yards

Wilbur Shaw wins the Indianapolis 500 in 4:22:31.201

Red Sox leftfielder Ted Williams pitches last 2 innings in loss to Tigers

Donald McNeill beat Bobby Riggs in US National Championship Men's Tennis

Leo Durocher suspended from Ebbetts Field for inciting a riot

Green Bay Packers become 1st NFL team to travel by plane

Four sets of brothers play in an NHL game Blackhawks vs Rangers

_____ / _____ / _____

___/___/___

___ / ___ / ___

___ /___ /___

_____ / _____ / _____

___ /___ /___

_____ / _____ / _____

___ /___ /___

_____ / _____ / _____

_____ / _____ / _____

___ / ___ / ___

___ /___ /___

____ / ____ / ____

___ /___ /___

_____ / _____ / _____

___ / ___ / ___

___ / ___ / ___

____ / ____ / ____

____ / ____ / ____

_____ /_____ /_____

___ /___ /___

_____ / _____ / _____

___ / ___ / ___

_____ / _____ / _____

_____ / _____ / _____

___ /___ /___

_____ / _____ / _____

___ / ___ / ___

_____ / _____ / _____

___ /___ /___

_____ / _____ / _____

___ /___ /___

___ / ___ / ___

___ /___ /___

___ / ___ / ___

___ / ___ / ___

___ / ___ / ___

_____ / _____ / _____

____ / ____ / ____

_____ / _____ / _____

_____ / _____ / _____

_____ /_____ /_____

_____ / _____ / _____

___ /___ /___

_____ / _____ / _____

_____ / _____ / _____

___ / ___ / ___

___ / ___ / ___

___ /___ /___

_____ / _____ / _____

_____ / _____ / _____

___ / ___ / ___

___ /___ /___

___ /___ /___

_____ / _____ / _____

___ / ___ / ___

___ / ___ / ___

___ /___ /___

___ /___ /___

_____ / _____ / _____

_____ / _____ / _____

___ / ___ / ___

_____ / _____ / _____

___ /___ /___

___ /___ /___

_____ / _____ / _____

___ / ___ / ___

___ / ___ / ___

_____ / _____ / _____

_____ / _____ / _____

_____ / _____ / _____

___ /___ /___

_____ / _____ / _____

___ / ___ / ___

___ /___ /___

___ / ___ / ___

_____ / _____ / _____

____ / ____ / ____

___ / ___ / ___

_____ / _____ / _____

_____ / _____ / _____

___ / ___ / ___

_____ / _____ / _____

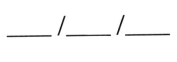

_____ / _____ / _____

_____ / _____ / _____

___ / ___ / ___

_____ / _____ / _____

___ / ___ / ___

___ / ___ / ___

_____ / _____ / _____

_____ / _____ / _____

___ /___ /___

___ / ___ / ___

___ / ___ / ___

___ / ___ / ___

___ / ___ / ___

___ /___ /___

___ / ___ / ___

_____ /_____ /_____

___ /___ /___

_____ / _____ / _____

_____ / _____ / _____

_____ / _____ / _____

___ / ___ / ___

_____ / _____ / _____

_____ / _____ / _____

____ /____ /____

_____ / _____ / _____

____ /____ /____

_____ / _____ / _____

_____ / _____ / _____

_____ / _____ / _____

___ / ___ / ___

_____ / _____ / _____

_____ / _____ / _____

Made in the USA
Columbia, SC
29 September 2022

68219393R00067